Publication Design by Amanda Jane Jones
Cover photograph by Young & Hungry

weldon**owen**

415 Jackson Street, Suite 200,
San Francisco, CA 94111
Telephone: 415 291 0100
Fax: 415 291 8841
www.wopublishing.com

Weldon Owen is a division of

**BONNIER**

# KINFOLK

# SUBSCRIBE

VISIT SHOP.KINFOLKMAG.COM

FOUR VOLUMES EACH YEAR

---

### CONTACT US

If you have any questions or comments,
email us at *info@kinfolkmag.com*

### SUBSCRIPTIONS

For questions regarding your subscription,
email us at *subscribe@kinfolkmag.com*

### STOCKISTS

If you would like to carry *Kinfolk*,
email us at *distribution@kinfolkmag.com*

### SUBMISSIONS

Send all submissions to
*submissions@kinfolkmag.com*

WWW.KINFOLKMAG.COM

# WELCOME

*We're all about celebrating the long-standing traditions we've always cherished, while also reminding ourselves to start a few of our own.*

When my parents blocked off two weeks on our summer calendar, I always knew what to expect. They would pack us in the family van for our annual trip to Echo Lake, Montana—perhaps the only place worthy of the long drive we'd endure together. I was eager to see summer friends and cousins, arriving ready to take on the card games and competitions for which I'd been training for months. We floated from dock to dock in our canoes and paddleboats, then spent our evenings challenging each other to midnight swims, just so we could float in the dark, looking back at the cabins.

This is where I pushed my adolescent limits—withstanding the heat before plunging, holding my breath while kicking to the bottom of the lake, skipping a rock one splash longer, and rising for an early morning swim. The routine was predictable, and we grew used to the same low-maintenance, high-yield meals from my mom and her friends; the goal was always to feed many mouths without jeopardizing their own time on the dock. These were my summers as I grew up, and the summer season was captured in this place.

Our stay at Echo Lake each year was an inexpensive trip for my parents; we'd always

travel with sandwiches and juice boxes for the road and arrive at a modest rental cabin—often shared with cousins. Frankly, I realize our family getaways could have been a lot more glamorous and exciting, but I respect that my parents found something that worked for us and committed to consistently making it happen each year.

The stories in this volume share ideas for creating summer traditions and travels, whether that means planning months in advance, or taking off for a last-minute weekend in the sun. Austin Sailsbury reminisces over the months he spent at summer camp in "Our Indian Summers," Nikaela Peters explores our tendency to migrate toward water in "Familiar Shores," and the Rhoads illustrate the spontaneity of a weekend on the road with their photo essay "Mountain Respite." We hope these stories will prompt you to try something new—or old—during the next few months. The meals and activities we promote with *Kinfolk* vary, but they are all based on our goal to create and strengthen relationships and to find more meaningful ways to connect and entertain. We're all about celebrating the long-standing traditions we've always cherished, while also reminding ourselves to start a few of our own.

**NATHAN WILLIAMS, EDITOR OF KINFOLK MAGAZINE**

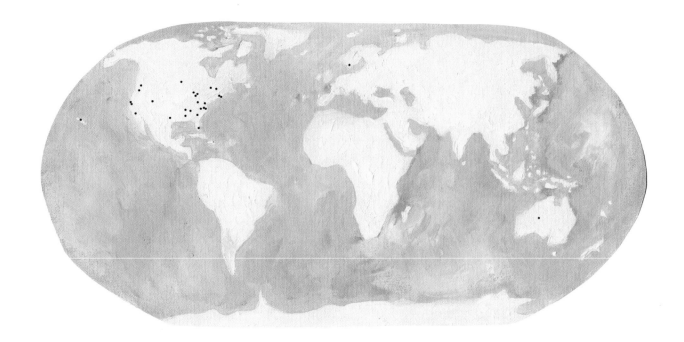

**NATHAN WILLIAMS**
*Editor*
*Portland, Oregon*

**AMANDA JANE JONES**
*Designer*
*Ann Arbor, Michigan*

**JULIE POINTER**
*Features Editor*
*Portland, Oregon*

**KATIE SEARLE-WILLIAMS**
*Features Editor*
*Portland, Oregon*

**ERICA MIDKIFF**
*Copy Editor*
*Birmingham, Alabama*

**JESSICA COMINGORE**
*Online Editor & Stylist*
*Los Angeles, California*

**KATIE STRATTON**
*Painter*
*Dayton, Ohio*

**PARKER FITZGERALD**
*Photographer*
*Portland, Oregon*

**ERIC ROSE**
*Photographer*
*Portland, Oregon*

**NIKAELA PETERS**
*Writer*
*Winnipeg, Canada*

**KYLIE TURLEY**
*Writer*
*Los Angeles, California*

**CAITLIN VAN HORN**
*Writer & Photographer*
*Birmingham, Alabama*

**NICO ALARY**
*Photographer & Writer*
*Australia*

**TEC PETAJA**
*Photographer*
*Nashville, Tennessee*

**JESSICA BAUCOM**
*Writer*
*Salt Lake City, Utah*

**REBECCA PARKER PAYNE**
*Writer*
*Richmond, Virginia*

**CHELSEA PETAJA**
*Stylist*
*Nashville, Tennessee*

**BRITT CHUDLEIGH**
*Photographer*
*Salt Lake City, Utah*

**ASHLEY PAQUIN**
*Writer*
*Portland, Oregon*

**REBECCA MARTIN**
*Writer*
*Blacksburg, Virginia*

**MICHAEL GRAYDON**
*Photographer*
*Toronto, Canada*

**NIKOLE HERRIOTT**
*Stylist & Photographer*
*Toronto, Canada*

**TARA O'BRADY**
*Writer*
*St. Catharines, Canada*

**WE ARE THE RHOADS**
*Photographers*
*Seattle, Washington*

**MARIA DEL MAR SACASA**
*Stylist*
*New York City, New York*

**EMMA ROBERTSON**
*Stylist*
*Los Angeles, California*

**EMILY KASTNER**
*Baker & Writer*
*Kalamazoo, Michigan*

**TIM ROBISON**
*Photographer*
*Asheville, North Carolina*

**MICHAEL MULLER**
*Photographer*
*Austin, Texas*

**SARAH VAN RADEN**
*Writer*
*Portland, Oregon*

**YOUNG & HUNGRY**
*Photographers*
*Los Angeles, California*

**KIRSTIN JACKSON**
*Writer*
*Oakland, California*

**MEGAN MARTIN**
*Writer*
*Palm Beach, Florida*

**JILL THOMAS**
*Photographer*
*San Diego, California*

**AUSTIN SAILSBURY**
*Writer*
*Denmark*

**GENTL & HYERS**
*Photographers*
*New York City, NY*

**JULIE & MATT WALKER**
*Filmmakers*
*Salt Lake City, Utah*

**WILLIAM HEREFORD**
*Photographer*
*Brooklyn, New York*

**RINNE ALLEN**
*Writer & Photographer*
*Athens, Georgia*

**ANITA BOHLERT**
*Writer*
*Portland, Oregon*

**LAURA D'ART**
*Photographer*
*Portland, Oregon*

**LEO PATRONE**
*Photographer*
*Salt Lake City, Utah*

**PAIGE BISCHOFF**
*Accountant*
*Portland, Oregon*

**CHELSEA FUSS**
*Writer & Stylist*
*Portland, Oregon*

**LISA WARNINGER**
*Photographer*
*Portland, Oregon*

**NICOLE FRANZEN**
*Photographer*
*Brooklyn, New York*

**MATTHEW REAMER**
*Photographer*
*San Francisco, California*

**DOUG BISCHOFF**
*Sales & Distribution*
*Portland, Oregon*

**TWILIGHT GREENAWAY**
*Writer*
*San Francisco, California*

**LEIF HEDENDAL**
*Cook & Stylist*
*San Francisco, California*

**SHANE POWERS**
*Stylist*
*New York City, New York*

**ALICE GAO**
*Photographer*
*Brooklyn, New York*

**CARISSA & ANDREW GALLO**
*Photographer, Filmmaker*
*Arlington, Virginia*

**SARAH SEARLE**
*Writer*
*Washington, DC*

**LIZZY SALL**
*Writer & Stylist*
*Brooklyn, New York*

**KAREN MORDECHAI**
*Photographer*
*Brooklyn, New York*

**ALPHA SMOOT**
*Photographer*
*New York City, New York*

# FEW

# ONE

ENTERTAINING FOR ONE

o

# THE PERFECT CUP: JENNI BRYANT

A BREWING SERIES BY NICO ALARY

*Jenni has no favorite origin; she simply loves the variety.*
*For her, a perfect cup is about the people who grew it, the place it was grown,*
*and how it made its way from there into her home.*

As I'm riding my bike down the streets of Brunswick, making my way past walls covered in colorful graffiti and through the Middle Eastern shops and restaurants, I'm wondering what the next couple of hours with Jenni are going to be like. I don't know her that well; I know that she is American and that, like me, she has done a fair bit of traveling. She's now part of the team of passionate coffee makers over at Market Lane, one of Melbourne's most respected cafés. Right turn on Davison Street, and Jenni's housemate is watering the garden on this hot January day. She invites me in. The house is gorgeous, the layout is original, the old hardwood floor creaks under my steps, there is a nice cool breeze coming from the backyard.

As she weighs the beans and rinses the paper filter, Jenni tells me she just moved in but already loves the place. I hand over my offering of almond croissants and pull out my camera as she starts grinding the beans, San Juan 8 Estrellas from Bolivia. When the water starts boiling, Jenni places her hand over the steaming water and says you can tell if the temperature is right based on the speed of the steam. I had no idea. A slow circular pour over the coffee grounds, and the first drops start to fill the glass jar; I can't help stepping closer to inhale deeply, a delicious smell emanating from the V60. I keep shooting as Jenni pours the coffee into the cups. The light is gorgeous, coming from the single window; the contrasts are almost Rembrandt-esque.

We take our cups to the garden and wander through the orange trees. We talk about how, just like the fruits in the garden, coffee is seasonal. Jenni has no favorite origin; she simply loves the variety. For her, a perfect cup is about the people who grew it, the place it was grown, and how it made its way from there into her home. The music stops and we go back inside to put on another record. The morning slowly goes by and coffee reveals one of its most amazing talents: connecting people and allowing two strangers to talk, to enjoy a simple moment. On this hot Friday morning in Brunswick, Jenni and I shared a cup of coffee, and we are strangers no more. ○

# RENAISSANCE JUICING

## OUR FAVORITE COMBINATIONS

A PHOTO ESSAY BY PARKER FITZGERALD & STYLING BY NATHAN WILLIAMS

*Carrot with a little ginger*

*Pear on ice*

*Apple, kale, and other greens*

*Sweet potato, ginger, orange, and carrot*

*Beet, apples, and greens*

*Oranges*

*Wheatgrass, grapefruit, orange, lemon and lime*

# A VISIT TO THE WOODSMAN MARKET

WORDS BY CHELSEA FUSS & PHOTOGRAPHS BY LISA WARNINGER

When a space opened between the original Stumptown Coffee and The Woodsman Tavern in Portland's SE Division Neighborhood, Duane Sorensen (owner of both establishments) took the opportunity to fill up the block. He opened a tiny food market focused on meats and cheeses, perhaps as a nod to his father, a butcher. Manager Carly Laws says the idea was to "open a neighborhood market and fill it with the things we like to eat—whatever is in our cupboards at home." Duane founded the world-famous artisanal coffee company, Stumptown, by visiting farms, finding the best coffee growers in the world, and talking with them face to face. This lack of middleman is also part of the philosophy of The Woodsman Market.

While spending an afternoon at the market, we noticed that suppliers and farmers stopped in throughout the afternoon, hand-delivering their goods. We met Ben Jacobsen, a salt vendor, who began selling salt just four months ago. After spending time in Norway and Denmark, where sea salt was much more accessible, Ben came back inspired to bring the best salt to the Northwest. Each week he rents a big truck with a 500-gallon tank, drives it to the coast, pumps the water from the ocean, and brings it back to Portland to process the salt. Jacobson's Salt is the only salt harvested in the Northwest, and it now sits proudly on the shelf next to Maldon salt, which is treasured by chefs for its light, flaky texture and subtle taste.

An Ibérico ham from Spain is a focal point in the shop, but it sits alongside meats and cheeses from Portland-area farms. Curated by Steve Jones, a Portland local who won the 2011 Cheesemonger Invitational in New York City, the cheese case is like the rest of the shop and includes a mix of Northwestern cheeses and the best from around the world. Every piece of merchandise is tested in their kitchens at home. Heinz ketchup sits next to imported tomatoes from Italy and peanuts made by a group of Methodist men in North Carolina. When I ask, "Why Heinz?" Carly says, "It's simply the best ketchup, so that's why we carry it." Noah, one of the managers, comments on their Oregon Tilth Certified Organic (OTCO) farm eggs, "Around our house we take eggs really seriously, so when it was time to buy them for the market, I knew exactly where to go. We know the chickens have had good lives. Scott brings us our eggs every Tuesday after lunch." The fresh chicken eggs sit in a wire basket inside a vintage cooler.

Inspired by travels to New York City and Amsterdam, Duane oversaw the design of the tiny grocery. Walls are splashed with subway tiles, weathered light fixtures hang above the counter, and vintage refrigerators hold eggs, herbs, and specialty drinks. Two antique carts sit in front of the shop. One holds produce, the other fresh flowers tucked into crockery pots. We were immediately struck by the effortlessness of the displays. Flower vendor Megan, of Fieldworks, notes that all the flowers come from local family farms. "Duane asked for the flowers to feel nonsensical and wild. He asked me to listen to Neil Young's Harvest as inspiration." Wild branches, local roses, and tiny seedlings fill the cart. It's hard to resist picking up a few stems along with some slices of prosciutto and provolone piccante for my dinner.

The food lovers at The Woodsman Market have managed to pack the best food from the Northwest and around the world into a tiny space that appears to be the sort of market you might only see in New York City. But they have bigger plans: Noah tells us they want to have a beehive on the roof to harvest honey, and Carly says they are scheming to make their own products. "We plan to create space in the back for pickling and making our own jams and jellies."

If you visit The Woodsman Market, you'll not only leave with delicious fare, you'll probably engage in conversation with a farmer or learn about how local salt is harvested. If you find yourself in Portland, OR, head straight over to SE Division for some Stumptown Coffee and a gander through this charming grocery. *Learn more at www.woodsmantavern.com*

# UNDOCUMENTED HOURS

WORDS BY REBECCA PARKER PAYNE & PHOTOGRAPHS BY NICO ALARY

*The past few years have levied a strange burden of proof upon our backs,*
*a burden to account for our hours and days, to prove to all who care to watch from the*
*screens of their phones and computers that we are doing something worthy with our*
*lives. In the meantime, we have forgotten how to be content in being present.*

Much of my time is spent in isolation, in the beauty of the silent, intimately tracing the ridges and ravines of my character. My time is also spent in community, where I find sacrifice and compassion, moving and charting the courses of friendships. In work also, through the wringing and gripping toil of my hands, I find contentment and confidence. But, I am an introvert without a camera. I am a friend without an audience. I am a baker without a blog. The cumulative collision of my life's meaning, the arching composition and texture that keep this heart beating, exist without any traces of documentation.

I know full well that beauty and art dwell here in these unseen places. And often, as a writer, and in a sense an artist, I feel compelled to share it, to prove that I am living an artist's life. Snap a photo, draw up a post, compose a quippy 140 characters—all to tangibly account for the many pinnacles of my productivity and accomplishment.

Yet, there is much at stake in this place. For in our isolation and in our community, there is a beauty born of intimacy, experienced through presence, and bound by trust. Inherently, this very experience would be betrayed by the manipulation of these moments to our artistic demands. Annie Dillard wrote that when we are fully present to an experience, when we see in a way that involves letting go, when we become holistically present, we stand "transfixed and emptied." [1]

The past few years have levied a strange burden of proof upon our backs, a burden to account for our hours and days, to prove to all who care to watch from the screens of their phones and computers that we are doing something worthy with our lives. In the meantime, we have forgotten how to be content in being present. We have not been transfixed and emptied since we first believed the lie that all of our experiences must be shared.

There is a chain of command here: we are at the bottom, and we glean inspiration where we can. We do not own our time, but stand under these whirling dervishes, hoping for a moment that is safe to share without removing us from the experience, and without imposing our own demands for the moment. Time dances brilliantly above us and around us. We only bestow the hems of her skirts for our tiny artistic visions.

Let us all remember, now in the presence of one another, that our memories are enough. May we live to remind each other to partake of dinner without pause for a clicking shutter or a scribbling pen. Stay here, drink more wine, and let the memories of a time exist by themselves within you, and between you and the others. And may your art be a sincere reflection of what already exists, not a post of projection for what we desire.

Keep your hours close, and keep intimacy and trust closer. If we give this a chance, we will surely realize that being present is powerful enough to burn and consume our hearts, minds, and memories with fullness unparalleled. ○

*But there is another kind of seeing that involves a letting go. When I see this way I sway transfixed and emptied.*
*The difference between the two ways of seeing is the difference between walking with and without a camera.*
*When I walk with a camera I walk from shot to shot, reading the light on a calibrated meter.*
*When I walk without a camera, my own shutter opens, and the moment's light prints on my own silver gut.*
*When I see this second way I am above all an unscrupulous observer.* [1]

---

ANNIE DILLARD, *PILGRIM AT TINKER CREEK*

# DINING FOR ONE

*Dining alone is sometimes thought of as an experience void of enjoyment,
or one that requires a list of rules. Experiencing the opposite can create a life
of pleasurable autonomy, and offers an opportunity to really get to know yourself.*

Dining and dating often go hand in hand, but how often do you dine solo and really enjoy—and thrive from—the experience? Dining alone is sometimes thought of as an experience void of enjoyment, or one that requires a list of rules. Experiencing the opposite can create a life of pleasurable autonomy, and offers an opportunity to really get to know yourself.

Everything you want to know about yourself can be found in your relationship with food. Food is comfort, pleasure, celebration, and relief; it is the one companion that never leaves or fails. Sometimes what we think we deserve is reflected in what we eat; might it be possible to change this by setting a place for one at the dinner table? Eating can be a time when you build the deepest relationship with yourself, and can be used as a doorway to discovery.

Curious about what it would be like to date yourself? Make a meal and draw up a chair for fun! Yes, it's lovely to spoil yourself at a fine restaurant, but cooking can provide a deeper connection with your food, and it gives you an opportunity to be completely driven by your own senses. When you cook for yourself, you let your own selfish tastes take over—you get to do, and be, exactly what you want.

Dig deep into your recipe coffers and forgo the convenience foods. Maybe this is a great reason to pull out the linen, polish the silver, wear your fine silk, and get close to the things that really fan your

fire. Let this date be a delicious way to coerce new desires and give you a reason to try new things. Nourishing yourself with fine bread, salt, and wine is by no means a priggish act; it should be done often. Dining alone can be a great way to celebrate what it means to feast on life—your life.

By setting the table and creating the stage, you invite a new openness that would not otherwise be there. When you move away from the external distractions of a busy dining room, the experience of cooking and enjoying a meal reaches the summit of perfection. A relationship is an anchor that always brings you back to something, loving or not. Explore the goods of your heart and do it in silence; try putting down the phone and switching off the internal radio station. Relationships have constant dialogue, even when words are unspoken, and your own subtle dialogue is waiting to be yoked with food and drink. Invite your creativity, anguishes, and richness; solitude has never been tastier or more fulfilling.

Perhaps dining alone is the perfect way to rethink your relationship with yourself, and to reconfigure the pathway to self and love. Creating intimacy alone—allowing the time and the room to have a tender relationship with yourself—encourages broader and deeper relationships and community with others. By cultivating the riches within, we can then share them far and wide, and the magic continues on.

WORDS BY ASHLEY PAQUIN & PHOTOGRAPH BY LEO PATRONE

*Warm nighttime breezes*

*Screen doors slapping*

*Late-night porch chats*

*The coldness of the river*

*Crickets*

*Open, screenless windows*

*Dogs at the park*

*Wild blackberries*

*Morning shadows through the curtain*

*Reading in the sun*

*Sand in my hair*

*Skin stretched tightly over my nose*

*Dust in my car from adventures*

*Eating fruit all day long*

*Dining on my stoop*

*The smell of backyard barbecues*

---

**KINFOLK SUMMER LIST**

# DINNER WITH KLAUS

INTERVIEW BY KYLIE TURLEY & PHOTOGRAPHS BY MICHAEL MULLER

**R**enowned architectural photographer Klaus Frahm recognizes the urgency to create meaningful bonds with friends and strangers alike. Intimate gatherings warmed by flickering candles and the smell of homemade foods is not a rarity in his Hamburg, Germany, home. Klaus redefines small gatherings by combining tradition and spontaneity to create something especially memorable.

---

### WHAT INSPIRES YOU TO COOK AND ENTERTAIN FOR FRIENDS?

Eating together creates an intimate connection between people. Similar to what you learn in the family as a young child, where nearly every day you eat together at the same table, it bonds people. I enjoy sharing these moments over food with friends, and it is much nicer to cook for others. I live alone with 350 square meters of living area. Space means possibilities, and this house is ideal to entertain. I like to have an open house. My grandfather had the same idea by inviting prisoners of war and refugees to supper. As the years passed, they always returned to my family because of our generosity and friendship. My parents mirrored my grandfather's example and frequently invited friends from the village to our home as well. This tradition continues because it is important to be friendly with everyone.

### THE FIRST PHOTO YOU TOOK WAS OF YOUR HOUSE. WHY DID YOU CHOOSE YOUR HOME?

I took my first photo with a box camera when I was nine years old. Since I was a very young child, I had a strong connection to the house. It was passed down from my grandfather to my father and then finally, to me. Every child has a connection to the home they are raised in—but this house is special. It is not very old, built in 1883, and I often tell myself, "Maybe I'm so crazy about the place because I once lived here." I often wonder if I could have been reincarnated from someone who had lived in the house before and therefore feel deeply connected to it.

### AS A CHILD, DID YOU HELP YOUR MOTHER IN THE KITCHEN?

Growing up on a farm, it was always necessary that the children help in the home during harvest. I started to bake when I was nine years old and wanted to learn how to make the family's favorite hazelnut cake. Hazelnut cake was always fun for all the children, and when my children grew up and had a birthday, I continued the tradition and baked the same hazelnut cake. Everybody loves the taste of that cake. My mother knew how to cook very well, and passed it on to me. Cooking is something to know for yourself. It is knowledge—pure survival. If you don't know how to cook, you're lost. If you always eat what other people cook it can be terrible because you never know what kind of mood the cook was in while preparing the dinner.

**HOW WOULD YOU DEFINE "ENTERTAINING"?**

To entertain is to bring people together by invitation to interact, share conversation, and make music. Creating music is natural. Since I was young, I have played guitar and piano. My son became an excellent pianist. In my home I have a grand piano standing in the living room and naturally, when somebody can play they should play. It is always nice to have live music. Its nonverbal communication can be a means to entertain guests.

I'm a very spontaneous person; I don't book in advance—I invite people with short notice and if I have luck, someone comes. If I have no luck, nobody comes. The guest list is always a mixture. People I know from work, even if not very deeply, and friends or foreigners come to eat at my house. When I have a gathering, I invite about fifty people and around thirty come. Sometimes people are already friends and others are strangers. In the end, everyone leaves having made a new friend.

**IF YOU HAD ONLY THIRTY MINUTES TO PREPARE AND HOST A MEAL FOR GUESTS, WHAT WOULD YOU MAKE?**

I can make a lot of things in thirty minutes. To keep things simple, I would prepare pasta with green asparagus—ingredients I always have on hand. First, wash the asparagus and peel the bottom 3–4 inches. Trim the ends and cut asparagus into pieces, leaving the tops aside. Meanwhile, sufficiently salted water is boiling in a pot or pan. Depending on the choice of pasta (penne or strozzapreti is best, not spaghetti), add pre-cooked pasta followed by asparagus. Pasta and asparagus are cooked in the same water. Asparagus takes about seven minutes to cook, and the tops five. When cooked al dente, put away the water and add fresh olive oil and black pepper. To serve, add fresh parmigiano and oil as desired. A bit of lemon—if at hand—is delicious, but be sure to add the lemon just prior to eating because it turns fresh green into olive green. Once the food is ready I would light the candles, put on dishes, and wait for the guests to arrive.

**IN REFERENCE TO YOUR WORK IN PHOTOGRAPHY YOU ONCE SAID, "WHERE THERE'S NO RISK, THERE'S NO FUN." DO YOU FIND THIS TO BE TRUE IN THE KITCHEN AS WELL?**

For sure! For example, I visited my friend who was ill and we decided to cook. He gave me pasta and a can of tomatoes. There was a grape vine on the table so I cut them up and added them to the pasta. Tomatoes and grapes are both fruits and with the right spices, make a winning combination. In cooking, you must take risks sometimes, always changing and experimenting to find the perfect blend. I don't read any recipe books—I cook from the heart, using knowledge and recipes that my mother taught me. Cooking and preparing is all timing. It's chaotic because my kitchen is so small that when I have guests and they ask, "Can I help you?" I say, "Oh yes, you can stand there in the doorway and watch." It's not perfect, but it's fun. ○

*First, wash the asparagus and peel the bottom 3–4 inches.*
*Trim the ends and cut asparagus into pieces, leaving the tops aside.*
*Meanwhile, sufficiently salted water is boiling in a pot or pan.*
*Depending on the choice of pasta (penne or strozzapreti is best, not spaghetti),*
*add pre-cooked pasta followed by asparagus. Pasta and asparagus are cooked in the same water.*
*Asparagus takes about seven minutes to cook, and the tops five.*
*When cooked al dente, put away the water and add fresh olive oil and black pepper.*

**PASTA WITH GREEN ASPARAGUS BY KLAUS FRAHM**

# TWO

ENTERTAINING FOR TWO

∘ ∘

# FAMILIAR SHORES

WORDS BY NIKAELA PETERS

PHOTOGRAPHS BY TEC PETAJA & STYLING BY CHELSEA PETAJA

*At the lake we don't mind that the shower keeps breaking
or that the stove never works properly—we have affection for the dumpy and rusty
and rickety things because we associate them with last summer, with childhood,
with feeling small and content in a big and slow-moving world.*

---

We're not so different from elephants. We travel in groups, we prioritize family, and like the elephants of Sri Lanka, we migrate annually toward water. Every year during the dry season, these elephants congregate with their families on the shores of Minneriya Lake. Researchers have noted that here, by the lake, the elephants renew old friendships and play together. They eat and flirt and bathe and drink. They are lazy. They swim in the sun, and rest in the shade. Like us, they are social and ritualistic and proud.

In many ways, our annual migration out of our urban lives to a familiar shore can be understood scientifically: the air is hot, the water is cool; cities are smoggy, the country is fresh; human eye muscles are most relaxed when settled on the horizon line; swimming is physically redemptive and psychologically meditative; beer tastes better on a dock. Perhaps, though, there is much that can't be so systematically reduced. Were we to be observed the way the elephants are, by researchers from a distance trying to better understand our peculiar habits, would they notice that we open up to each other when we spend a few days in a cabin? How conversation gets easier and relationships strengthen? Would they notice how lying on our backs on the dock at night reminds us of when we were kids? Would they notice that we fret less about what and when we are going to eat, but more regularly and eagerly gather around food? Would they notice that our tendencies change: that we read more, sleep more, fuss less over details?

At the lake we don't mind that the shower keeps breaking or that the stove never works properly—we have affection for the dumpy and rusty and rickety things because we associate them with last summer, with childhood, with feeling small and content in a big and slow-moving world. We love the lake partly because it is not our home. Like the elephants, we accept that our life cannot always be so idle, leisurely, and peaceful. We accept that we can't always play cards until 2 a.m., skinny dip under the stars, and live off avocado sandwiches and pickles. Yet, like the elephants during dry season, we indulge for a couple of weeks each year in this necessary luxury, and return to ordinary city life more at home and more alive. ○ ○

# INN BY THE SEA

### WORDS AND PHOTOGRAPHS BY RINNE ALLEN

A night spent at the Marston House leaves a lasting impression. Inspiring spaces and heartfelt details introduce guests to a distinct approach to living: a breakfast left by the door in a wicker basket, a simple fireplace to warm the room, a garden to enjoy and embrace. One cannot help getting lost in these considered gestures.

Seamlessly, the lines blur between public and private spaces. A garden path leads from the guest-house to the innkeepers' home and shop. Once inside, room leads to room; in one, a kitchen door is open, the threshold between shop and home.

Proprietors Sharon and Paul Mrozinski gravitated to the Maine coast over twenty-five years ago by way of the west. They equally felt the pull of New England, of its "water, green trees, and seasons." On one early visit, an abandoned sea captain's house on Main Street in Wiscasset beckoned. The property appealed to the architect in Paul and the shopkeeper in Sharon. They both recognized within themselves a dream of living and working within the walls of the home. They have spent the past twenty-five years cultivating a lifestyle of honest simplicity that is a gift to all who visit, whether for an hour or a weekend.

### BITS OF WISDOM FROM SHARON & PAUL

"We had spent some time looking into the windows of this eighteenth-century sea captain's home in the dead center of the village, wondering why was it abandoned. That is how we came to find and buy The Marston House."

"We live our lives honestly and simply—utility, authentic, natural, heartfelt—filled with the spirit of the one that created it. We love the hard work of 'homemade,' the individual signature which is stamped into anything made by hand; you may not see it, but will feel it."

"Whatever Paul and I do we do for ourselves, hoping our guests will like what we like."

"After finding the perfect basket and discovering that everything fits into it, we knew it would be a delight to fill, to serve, and to receive. Who wouldn't love a basket filled with fresh-baked biscuits, homemade granola, and fruit delivered to you for breakfast?"

"We pick our 'spaces' with specific needs: to have a beautiful view even if it is only of the garden, a fireplace to enjoy body and soul, an abundance of natural light. We keep as much history of place as we possibly can, and no televisions or telephones or distractions from the day-to-day rigors each of us experience. "

"To please ourselves and in the process pleasing our guests, we offer them a place of deep comfort. We want our clients 'to feel special and that they are the wanted and expected guests.' If we can convey this feeling then we believe we are successful in offering hospitality."

# BELLOCQ TEA ATELIER

INTERVIEW BY KATIE SEARLE-WILLIAMS & PHOTOGRAPHS BY GENTL & HYERS

**WHERE DID THE IDEA TO START BELLOCQ TEA ATELIER COME FROM?**

The idea started as two separate projects. Michael was very interested in designing an extraordinary tabletop experience. I had a deep appreciation for fine teas—the teas that you find, and fall in love with, when you're traveling. I originally envisioned sharing my love of the poetic tea experience in the form of a book. After about nine months of consideration, Bellocq was the offspring from these two projects.

**WHAT ARE THE INSPIRATIONS FOR YOUR BLENDS?**

Bellocq Blends are often inspired by two elements: our rich selection of pure teas and poetics. When we source teas, we purchase the teas we love, the ones that excite and surprise us, the teas that have a richness and depth of flavor. We have great respect for the teas and their natural flavors. The flavor profiles of these pure teas often tell us what they want to become. But sometimes I am driven to blend a tea inspired by riding horses in the snow-covered mountains.

**THERE IS SOMETHING DEEPER AND MORE POIGNANT ABOUT YOUR APPROACH TO BELLOCQ THAN JUST A TEA SHOP; WHAT WOULD YOU SAY THAT IT IS?**

We know the essence of Bellocq exists but we don't know quite what it is. We have many ideas and these ideas help us understand the essence of Bellocq—what Bellocq is like—but these ideas have never indicated exactly what Bellocq is. We all see Bellocq as having a spirit of it's own. In terms of taste and style it doesn't belong to any one of us, but we understand what it needs (experience) and what it wants (romance).

**WHAT SETS ANY BUSINESS APART IS THEIR STORY.**
**CAN YOU BRIEFLY OUTLINE YOUR JOURNEY FROM THE BEGINNING TO WHERE YOU ARE NOW?**

Bellocq was initially envisioned opening somewhere in NYC. We were searching for spaces in NYC, however Scott found the perfect space...in London. So we were surprisingly and excitely off to Great Britain. London is a great city; we love the restrained romance, the structure of their elegance, the richness and layering of their culture. Bellocq has a rigor that was a great fit with London. It felt like we had always been there and could somehow always remain there. While in London we found a second, larger space in Brooklyn where we would be able to create our blends. After a year in London we lost our space and could not spare the resources to relocate and rebuild. So here we are, loving Brooklyn but deeply desiring the next adventure.

**THERE IS OBVIOUSLY A GREAT DEAL OF INNOVATION INVOLVED IN THE DECISIONS FOR**
**AND OPERATIONS OF YOUR TEAM. WHAT WOULD YOU SAY IS THE INSPIRATION AND DRIVING**
**FORCE FOR THE DECISIONS YOU ULTIMATELY MAKE?**

On the operations side we believe all good decisions are the product of inspiration paired with appropriate timing. This does not mean waiting, since we believe inspired ideas often require immediate effort.

**WHAT EXPERIENCE DO YOU INTEND AND HOPE FOR YOUR CUSTOMERS TO HAVE**
**WHEN ENCOUNTERING BELLOCQ?**

Our clients are our guests. We are here to graciously share extraordinary teas. We want each client to love the teas they select and to enjoy the process.

**DO YOU HAVE A MANIFESTO OR MISSION STATEMENT THAT YOU OPERATE BY**
**AND TRANSMIT THROUGH YOUR DAILY ACTIONS?**

I'll make one up for you: "Don't forget love."

**WHAT DO YOU FORESEE FOR BELLOCQ IN THE FUTURE?**

Bellocq will be enjoyed by the best clients, regardless of their geographic location. ○ ○

# ETERNITY IN AN AFTERNOON

*I sweep up the baby and we sit, together, snuggled in the armchair by the dining room window. She is warm and soft, still halfway between sleep and waking.*

"The days are long," say other moms who see me toting my baby around. "But the years are short," they always add. They mean *carpe diem*, or something like it: this time won't last forever, so enjoy the moments while she's still small. But in my experience, the days fly. Between lifting her out of her crib at daybreak and laying her down for the night, I feel like I'm chasing down the clock.

I pull her from the crib, change her diaper and her clothes (sometimes twice, if I'm unlucky), and head for the kitchen. I'm always surprised: eight-thirty already? But the glowing green numbers on the stovetop don't lie. Breakfast is a longer meal than it used to be, and I'm learning to savor the calm time with my daughter; the *carpe diem* lesson applies here. But then we're off to play, and in no time it seems, to sleep again: morning nap. If I'm disciplined, I write. I fill up an hour and a half with words and imaginings. Otherwise, I twiddle the time away on food prep and house straightening and blogs and emails. Either way, the wake-up cry sounds from below sooner than I expect, and I'm down to the baby's room for diapering, lunch, errands, more play if we can squeeze it in, and then another nap, the afternoon one.

Here is where the hours begin to stretch out. I allow myself a couch sit and a drink: coffee if it's an early nap, wine if it's later. I read, I doze, I watch something on the BBC and stitch on an embroidery piece that's been lying around for several months. And I start to feel antsy. Nap time is me time, and yes, I savor it. But now I grow a little lonely, especially in the waning afternoon light. I wander the upstairs indecisively. I go down to the kitchen and heat up milk. I make sure the sippy cup is washed and ready. I check the stovetop clock. I actually stalk the nursery door. And then I hear it! The first peep of waking.

I sweep up the baby and we sit, together, snuggled in the armchair by the dining room window. She is warm and soft, still halfway between sleep and waking. She drinks her afternoon milk and leans into me. I give her a squeeze and look out the window, lit by white lights from the inside and a sunset glow from the outside.

"Never wake a sleeping baby," everyone says. But for this, I would. This is our tradition. This is my favorite part of the day. The time may fly, but this is the moment I want to keep for eternity.

WORDS BY REBECCA MARTIN & PHOTOGRAPH BY ERIC ROSE
STYLED BY SARAH VAN RADEN

# OF FEAST AND FIELD

**WORDS AND PHOTOGRAPHS BY CAITLIN VAN HORN**

Woven into the very fibers of our being is the need to retreat, to slow down and connect with something or someone that was once lost: the innocence of our youth, an estranged loved one, the wild abandon of a summer's day. All are memories that slowly abate until one morning we wake up, relinquish the necessities of the day, and make it our ambition to find what was lost and hold it steadfastly.

There was once a young couple flanked with responsibilities, leaden with distractions, burdened with exhaustion, and hungry for days of old. Deeper they tilled, foraging their hearts like a wren in the woods, longing to find what was missing in the staleness of the day. It didn't take long for the memory to swell of a favorite pastime long forgotten. A walk through the woods bowered with moss and fern to an open field where once they spent idle days in each other's arms.

As the faded memory flickered in the corner of their minds, they realized what they had to do: abandon the myriad of responsibilities and return to that warm summer's day to steal back what time had so cruelly taken from them.

Immediately they busied themselves, gathering the essentials needed for a day away from home. A feast was in order—a communion of delicacies to grace the plate and palate, all carefully wrapped in cheesecloth and twine. Before long an array of charcuterie, fine breads, and accompanying sides dressed the table. It was a meal to bring together two souls, strong enough to awaken two hearts and resurrect memories suppressed. Picnic in hand, they set out for their field.

The drive was peaceful, hands entwined, half-moon grins, hair tousled by the warm summer breeze. The sweet aroma of jasmine scented the air while gossamer swayed from nearby branches. Minds were at rest and were comforted by the cooing meadowlarks. Through a forested cove they emerged at the field of their paled recollection. A wave of emotion and nostalgia came like a flood. They had arrived.

They settled into a cozy nook. Easily, the conversation flowed; all tension and insecurities faded. Joyfully they inhaled their vittles whilst gazing out among a field of clover and wild grass. The loamy soil was soft, peppered with red Alabama clay. Mustard blooms were picked, pictures were taken, kisses shared, sweet moments treasured. Hours were spent until the hazy sun made its slow decent.

Lying there in each other's arms, bellies swollen with content, the young couple relished every moment, yearning for time to slow its course. But in their hearts they knew tomorrow was fast approaching, and before long the routine demands of the day would set in. They promised each other to never forget that day, the field, the meal, the love.

What once was lost had been found and remains, held ever so closely to the breast, a memory cherished and a reminder that when life gets in the way, a feast and a field await.

# ADAM AND CHELSEA JAMES

## TRAVEL & HOME EXCHANGES AS A YOUNG FAMILY

WORDS BY JESSICA BAUCOM

PHOTOGRAPHS BY BRITT CHUDLEIGH

*I like to be able to stay somewhere and be able to get to know it really well.*
*I like to ride my bike around and get to know the shops and the bakeries—something*
*a bit more intimate.*

From the moment Chelsea and Adam met, the concept of home had a whole new meaning. "The first thing we did (after we were married) was go on a six-month honeymoon," Adam explains. "We went to London, bought a van, and took it across the continent. We drove everywhere. Chelsea had never been to Europe, which was like a sin in my eyes, so we had to go right away." Chelsea says, "I thought, 'We can't just go to Europe and live in a car; you're crazy.' But then we went over there and we did it. We didn't have any plans whatsoever, and it all worked out and it was such an adventure." She adds candidly, "We got to know each other really fast."

This European road trip was only the beginning of the unconventional traveling ahead for the Jameses. Since their marriage in the summer of 2004, Chelsea and Adam have been to five different continents, over fifty countries, and taken endless amounts of flights, train rides, and road trips.

Living on the road suited the young couple. As an artist, Chelsea was flexible about where and when she could work, and Adam could run his online business from any location with wifi. "Home" became an ever-evolving combination of new destinations. The couple rarely looked at their travels as a vacation—there was always a motivating factor. "For us, it's less about 'Let's go on vacation.' It's more like, 'Let's go get inspiration.'" Chelsea adds, "We work from home, so we get burnt out; when I need a break, we go take a break; then I am ready to work again."

Chelsea and Adam's life in the States mirrored their transient lifestyle abroad for a while—living in multiple states and in multiple homes seemed like a natural way of life—but eventually the reality of moving furniture and belongings became exhausting. They had an added incentive to settle down when they learned they were expecting; they found the perfect place to settle, and Lulu arrived in February 2010.

Having a new baby brought many of the typical lifestyle changes for these two, but it did not bring Chelsea and Adam's need to travel to a halt—not even close. They knew, however, that something would have to change. "…Living in a car with Lulu? It wouldn't be fun; it would be hard," Chelsea says. The solution? A home exchange, something Adam heard about from another traveler. People swap homes for an agreed amount of time, each using the other's spaces like their own.

Adam admits he was skeptical at first. "I think everyone, when they first hear about it, is kind of nervous. Someone living in my house—how do you trust them?" But as they did their research, they realized the participants were just like them: people looking for a unique trip that would give them an inside perspective on how others live across the world.

"We're at a new stage. I like to be able to stay somewhere and be able to get to know it really well. I like to ride my bike around and get to know the shops and the bakeries—something a bit more intimate," Chelsea explains. Adam goes on, "People in this program take a lot of pride in telling you about their favorite restaurant or their favorite places around town. We've had experiences where their friends even come over and want to take us around and have us over for dinner; it's really remarkable."

Since participating in home exchanges through a program called HomeLink, the Jameses have stayed in France, the Netherlands, Sweden, and New York City. "Amsterdam was my favorite." Chelsea remembers. "It was a five-story apartment on the canal." They receive requests for home exchanges "at least once a week," Adam explains. "I just responded to one in Paris. I had to say no of course, with the twins coming." (Yes, you heard right—Chelsea and Adam are now expecting twins!). When asked if the twins' arrival would slow down travel plans for a while, you can guess the answer: not a chance.

So what advice does this adventurous couple have for all of us who long to travel? "Do it and do it now. Don't wait because the inspiration and the way it changes your life from the moment you get back is so important. Get that inspiration and change yourself for the better now instead of waiting and going when you really don't have the ability to change your life in such a drastic manner." ○ ○

# BROOKLYN BREAKFAST

*For just that brief spell, a breeze comes off the river and
we forget that in a few short hours we'll be wiping sweat from our brows,
frantically fanning ourselves with the morning paper.*

If you've ever been to Penn Station or the JFK airport on a Friday summer afternoon, you know the effect a hot New England sun has on city residents.

We flee.

Destinations vary, but transportation hubs look the same: a sea of gold-rimmed Ray-Bans, white canvas bags, and tan Rainbows. We'll take any lake, ocean, pool, or mountain for a fresh breeze and solace from that sizzling pavement.

A two-day break recharges us, allows us to face that urban sauna all over again. Some of us, however, are not so lucky every weekend. Some of us have longer stretches with no respite from extreme temperatures and extreme smells.

Our secret trick to making it all bearable? Calm, quiet mornings.

Sunrise is the only time when the streets of the city belong to us—like there is one key for entry, and it's in our pocket. At sunrise the pavement has cooled and the streets have calmed. Near the water in Brooklyn we trick ourselves even more: we watch the sun as it kisses Manhattan good morning, and reflects down on our East River. We sit quietly with the cool breeze and forget that it's ever any different.

When life permits, we pack an easy breakfast in the dark with cold ingredients from the fridge. Hard-boiled egg with crisp cool greens, fresh avocado, pesto from last night's dinner, all on a store-bought brioche roll. We throw summer's ripest berries in a jar with some mint and raw sugar, and tuck in some powdered donuts. We bottle cold coffee brewed yesterday, and freshly squeezed grapefruit juice.

We can't think of a better way to start our day or revive our senses. For a minute we believe we're the only people in Brooklyn. For just that brief spell, a breeze comes off the river and we forget that in a few short hours we'll be wiping sweat from our brow, frantically fanning ourselves with the morning paper.

WORDS BY LIZZY SALL & PHOTOGRAPH BY KAREN MORDECHAI
STYLING BY KAREN MORDECHAI & LIZZY SALL OF SUNDAY SUPPERS

# INTO THE BEGUILING WILD

## AN ODE TO THE DARKEST OF THE YEAR'S BRIGHTEST SEASON

WORDS BY TARA O'GRADY & PHOTOGRAPHS BY MICHAEL GRAYDON & NIKOLE HERRIOTT

*There is, in the lush, emerald shadows, the suggestion of exploration*
*that beckons us into the beguiling wild.*

There is an ease in summer's days, in dressing in flips and shorts and well-worn cotton t-shirts. In driving with windows open, and in sleeping that way too. It is possible, and perfect, to rise and retire with the sun. To eat outdoors.

That said, we think the magic of the season becomes truly evident—is at its full effect—in the study of its contrasts. Too much brightness blinds the eye. Too much dimness dulls the senses.

But dark and light in conversation? Now *there's* the thing.

The throaty bite of olive oil is galvanized by fennel's high-noted fragrance. Plunging into cool ocean water is especially bracing when your skin is prickled flush with sunshine. The swallowed effervescence of beer is a revelation on a night when the air is heavy with humidity, thick and drinkable. The crunch of a spicy, peppery cookie giving way to the smooth sweet of ice cream shows each at its best.

In summer the landscape opens up and draws us in, coming alive with mysteries: the sound of cicadas giving song to the lucent indigo of evening. The melodies of birds in the pearlized blush of morning, granting company. There are whispers of adventures afoot. There is, in the lush, emerald shadows, the suggestion of exploration that beckons us into the beguiling wild.

It is a lure that pulls us off beaten trails, inspires the desire to turn down new roads, to kneel in black earth to plant and harvest our meals, to take to waters to catch our suppers. It bolsters bravery, and leads us to find beauty in the sequined, silver flash of a salmon's tail with the wet brown of a dock as backdrop. Summer is when the out-of-doors is at its most hospitable.

And it suits us fine.

Not far from where we live there is a craggy outcrop of an escarpment that is covered by a forest. In winter, it is a formidable obstacle: a white and grey geometry of stone and tree trunks ramrod straight. In autumn and spring we walk there when we can, but the rains often make the slopes irregular and treacherous. Waters rush by at a dangerous speed, and there is an undercurrent of quiet uncertainty to the excursion. But in summer, welcoming summer, the rocks are soft-edged with moss. The forest floor is bouncy with fresh shoots and enthusiastic blooms; the twisted angles of branches are laced by bud and leaf.

In there, somewhere, at the right time, there are black raspberries. Tiny, less than the size of my pinky's fingernail, they're deep and beaming all at once, muskily tannic in a way that suits a home of brambles and thorn. They have the specific taste of the untamed.

To us, that is summer. ○ ○

**CAMPFIRE SALMON**

*Lightly cured in sugar and salt, scented by dill,*
*then grilled as you like*


**JADEITE SALAD**

*Shaved fennel, segmented pomelo and its juice,*
*avocado, and a crunchy sprinkle of fennel seeds*


**STICK TWIST BREAD**

*Quick bread toasted over hot coals until*
*smoky and crisp*


**GINGERSNAP SANDWICHES**

*Vanilla bean ice cream and berries smushed*
*in between homemade gingersnap biscuits*


**MARIONBERRY SIP**

*Marionberry-infused vodka, simple syrup, and*
*mint, bubbly with soda*

# CAMPFIRE SALMON

### RECIPE BY TARA O'BRADY & NIKOLE HERRIOTT

A simple rub of sugar and salt layered with dill adds an aromatic, herbaceous depth to salmon that's later grilled over a hot fire. Even though the seasoning is washed away, the light cure of the sugar helps the fish develop a truly burnished exterior, and where it's licked by the flames, the flesh and fat get exceptionally charred.

½ cup granulated sugar

¼ cup coarse sea salt

1 teaspoon black pepper, freshly ground

1 large bunch fresh dill, picked from stems

2–3 pounds fresh side of salmon, pinboned and scaled, but skin on

2 tablespoons butter, melted

Fresh dill and lemon wedges to serve

**INSTRUCTIONS** In a medium bowl, stir together the sugar, salt, and pepper. In a dish large enough to hold the fish, sprinkle half the sugar mixture over the bottom of the dish along with a few pieces of dill. Place the salmon, skin side down, on top of the seasoning. Lay the rest of the dill over the flesh of the fish, then evenly distribute remaining sugar mixture on top. Cover the dish with cling film and refrigerate for 2 hours.

Preheat a grill or prepare a fire to medium-high heat. Lift the salmon from the seasonings, brushing off any that stick. Rinse the sides gently under running water and pat dry. Brush the salmon with some of the melted butter.

Lay the salmon on the grill, skin side down, leaving it alone without poking or prodding for a good 4 minutes. Baste the salmon with melted butter. With a large, thin spatula, flip the salmon over. Baste the skin with melted butter. Continue to grill until the salmon is almost cooked through, about 3 minutes more (see note below).

Carefully remove the fish from the grill and place, flesh side up, on a large platter or board, along with extra dill and lemon wedges. *Serves 4 generously, 6 nicely.*

**NOTE** If the salmon is freshly caught from the wild, which is our preference, it can be cooked to medium-rare with a hum of blushing pink through its middle (following instructions as given). If the salmon is farmed, or wild but not straight from the water, grill until opaque all the way through, but still moist—about 4–5 minutes per side.

Alternatively, the salmon can be cooked on a soaked (untreated) cedar plank if you have some knowledge of how to manage such a method, and have a board kicking about that is thick and sturdy and suitable. The salmon should not be flipped in this scenario, but instead lidded or tented with foil to cook through.

# STICK TWIST BREAD

**RECIPE BY TARA O'BRADY & NIKOLE HERRIOTT**

**W**e just might crave this bread more than toasted marshmallows…well, maybe not, but it's close. The crust goes crisp and singes in a way we like, and the crumb is soft and springy. It's quick work to bring the dough together, which affords a satisfying sense of accomplishment through minimal effort. Butter or lard can be used instead of the bacon drippings, or even a neutral oil in a pinch.

Cooking sticks that are thin but sturdy work best, and they must be green (fresh) to prevent cooking fires. The bark may be whittled away, or left on and brushed clear of any loose bits or visible dirt.

---

2 ½ cups all-purpose flour

(plus more for dusting)

2 teaspoons baking powder

1 teaspoon raw sugar

½ teaspoon coarse sea salt

¼ cup bacon drippings, cold

½ cup milk

½ cup water, approximately

---

**METHOD** In a decent-sized bowl, whisk together the flour, baking powder, sugar, and sea salt. With two knives or a pastry cutter, cut the bacon fat into the dry mix, as you would when making biscuits. Keep cutting the fat until it is evenly distributed. Stir in the milk, and only enough water for the mixture to come together into a dough, using more or less water as needed.

Turn the dough out onto a lightly floured surface and knead gently until smooth. With a floured pin roll the dough into to a 1/4 inch thickness. Using a pastry cutter or sharp knife, cut the dough into 8 strips. Wrap one strip of dough around a prepared stick, starting at the top of the stick and twisting around and down, like the stripe on a candy cane. Continue wrapping the remaining pieces of dough, each around a new stick.

Toast the bread over hot coals rather than high flames, so that the heat is able to reach the center of the dough before the outside burns; rotate the stick often to ensure even cooking. The bread will be done when it has a deeply golden exterior and sounds hollow when tapped—around 5 minutes, depending on the heat and how thinly the dough was rolled.

Eat immediately, greedily. With butter is your best bet. *Makes 8 pieces.*

# FEW

ENTERTAINING FOR A FEW

○ ○ ○

# MOUNTAIN RESPITE

PHOTOGRAPHY BY SARAH & CHRIS RHOAD OF WE ARE THE RHOADS

When I was very young and the urge to be someplace else was on me, I was assured by mature people that maturity would cure this itch. When years described me as mature, the remedy prescribed was middle age. In middle age I was assured that greater age would calm my fever and now that I am fifty-eight perhaps senility will do the job. Nothing has worked. Four hoarse blasts of a ship's whistle still raise the hair on my neck and set my feet to tapping. The sound of a jet, an engine warming up, even the clopping of shod hooves on pavement brings on the ancient shudder, the dry mouth and vacant eye, the hot palms and the churn of stomach high up under the rib cage. In other words, I don't improve; in further words, once a bum always a bum. I fear the disease is incurable. I set this matter down not to instruct others but to inform myself.

When the virus of restlessness begins to take possession of a wayward man, and the road away from here seems broad and straight and sweet, the victim must first find in himself a good and sufficient reason for going. This to the practical bum is not difficult. He has a built-in garden of reasons to choose from. Next he must plan his trip in time and space, choose a direction and a destination. And last he must implement the journey. How to go, what to take, how long to stay. This part of the process is invariable and immortal. I set it down only so that newcomers to bumdom, like teen-agers in new-hatched sin, will not think they invented it.

Once a journey is designed, equipped, and put in process; a new factor enters and takes over. A trip, a safari, an exploration, is an entity, different from all other journeys. It has personality, temperament, individuality, uniqueness. A journey is a person in itself; no two are alike. And all plans, safeguards, policing, and coercion are fruitless. We find after years of struggle that we do not take a trip; a trip takes us. Tour masters, schedules, reservations, brass-bound and inevitable, dash themselves to wreckage on the personality of the trip. Only when this is recognized can the blown-in-the-glass bum relax and go along with it. Only then do the frustrations fall away. In this a journey is like marriage. The certain way to be wrong is to think you control it. I feel better now, having said this, although only those who have experienced it will understand it.[2]

---

**JOHN STEINBECK, EXCERPT FROM *TRAVELS WITH CHARLEY***

# BAKING SURPLUS

*There's a sweet exhilaration as I line them up on the cooling racks;*
*I'm not quite sure where they'll all end up.*

I've learned to love waking up early in the morning, before it's too hot and the summer sun has overrun everything. The moist night air still lingers, and the floor is hard and refreshingly cold to my bare feet. The heat of the oven doesn't seem like an affront to mankind at that hour, and the quiet of the early morning is a peaceful backdrop to a diligent culinary endeavor. My fingers must be nimble even though functioning so early isn't easy; nothing can drop on the floor—I'm sharing this food with others, after all.

I'm not sure why it hadn't crossed my mind at the very beginning—when I first set out to bake every single thing in a cookbook for my blog, Tar-Tryin'—but it wasn't until I found myself staring at a dozen croissants, fresh from the oven, that I realized how much food I was going to make over the next year.

The happy consequence of baking more is sharing more. Of course, hoarding an entire chocolate hazelnut tart is tempting; slowly eating my way through a cherry *clafoutis* seems quite appealing; and, while watching croissants rise in the oven, I certainly contemplate just how many I could possibly consume. Maybe not a *dozen* of them, but *at least* three or four. (Perhaps even five or six if they were spread out over the day.) All gluttony aside, the real and honest joy of baking is sharing food with people. To attain this satisfaction, it's not necessary to embark on a year-long project, nor is it necessary to plan an entire feast. A few hours in the kitchen whipping up something like a tray of strawberry *galettes* can lead to endless possibilities.

The aroma of these rustic, open-faced pies fills the air as I open the oven, and the ruby-hued juice bubbles over the edge of some of the flaky crusts. There's a sweet exhilaration as I line them up on the cooling racks; I'm not quite sure where they'll all end up. Some pastries are meant to be sweetly wrapped and left on a porch or with a neighbor who is celebrating one of life's milestones. There are also baked goods that call for gatherings—both planned and impromptu—where slicing into a pie or a tart requires a circle of friends. These *galettes* call for evening dessert on the porch, everyone relaxing and indulging as the heat of the day barely hangs on.

Most baked goods are best consumed fresh from the oven. It didn't take long for my kitchen surplus to turn into packed dinner tables and friends stopping by to scope out what might be cooling on the countertop. This surplus of baked goods has been a welcome adjustment to our daily lives; it's become standard—a staple—in our house. It's a beautiful life lesson for our son, and all of us really: we make food to share with those we love. It's always nice to enjoy a *galette*, but it's even more exciting to eat one with a friend, a brief delight that brings us together. So, bake more to share more—whatever that looks like in your life. You're bound to reap the joy of baking, the pleasure of enjoying food with friends, and an onslaught of praise and flattery. And who in their right mind doesn't enjoy a compliment?

WORDS BY EMILY KASTNER & PHOTOGRAPH BY TIM ROBISON

# HOW TO BE NEIGHBORLY

As is often the case, it's the little things that make all the difference. The tradition of borrowing and lending between neighbors in certainly not a new concept, and exchanges such as these are beneficial to both parties; they create a causal atmosphere of sharing and giving that is often lost in our busy lives. You never know what type of friendship you may create by reaching out to a neighbor. Here are some suggestions for cultivating a wonderful relationship.

### OFFER KIND GIFTS

· Drop off a cup of steaming coffee on your way to work.

· Take over an extra few cookies when you make a full batch.

· Deliver a warm basket of eggs, a freshly cut bunch of flowers, a loaf of hot bread from the oven.

· Take over a bowl of soup or a cup of tea when you know they aren't well.

### LEAVE THOUGHTFUL MESSAGES

· "Sorry to miss you; hope to see you soon!"

· "Thanks for watering our garden. Please enjoy some tomatoes!"

· "I picked far too many apples; here are a few especially pretty ones for your family to enjoy."

· "Headed for a walk to the community garden around 3 p.m.—care to join?"

### HELP AROUND THEIR HOUSE OR GARDEN

· Offer to water their garden or to feed their pets when your neighbor is out of town.

· Give them a few leftover seeds from your planting packets.

· Keep treats around for your neighbor's dog for when they visit.

### BORROW AND LEND HOUSEHOLD STAPLES

· Ask to borrow a few eggs and when you return the basket, be sure to tuck in a sweet thank you and a little treat—a small chocolate, a warm muffin, or a few eggs to replace the ones you borrowed.

· Lend your neighbor a tool they are in need of for a household repair. They may surprise you when you realize that you are out of nails, and they have just the ones.

### BE CONSIDERATE

· If your motion-sensitive night-light shines right in their bedroom window, offer to change the direction it illuminates.

· Don't throw loud parties, especially if they aren't invited.

WORDS BY SARAH VAN RADEN & ANITA BOHLERT
PHOTOGRAPHS BY MICHAEL MULLER

# ODE TO SUMMER'S CATCH

WORDS BY KIRSTIN JACKSON & PHOTOGRAPHS BY YOUNG & HUNGRY

STYLING BY JESSICA COMINGORE

*When the sun shines on my face as I sit on warm sand,*
*finishing the first of many relaxed courses of stone fruit or grilled fish,*
*it feels like time is holding deliciously still.*

---

**B**inds loosen in summer. The firm start times of winter dinners are left behind, and gatherings transition from beginning to end as gently and slowly as the season's sky fades into twilight. It's during these unhurried months that I hold dear the days spent at the beach with friends, sharing unfussy food. When the sun shines on my face as I sit on warm sand, finishing the first of many relaxed courses of stone fruit or grilled fish, it feels like time is holding deliciously still.

A northern Californian, I grew up knowing that the Pacific will not be any more welcoming or the water any more inviting just because it's summer. So I plan for a day when it will be. I wait until the air feels its absolute driest and the sun threatens to turn my green tomatoes red. Then, when it's hot enough to fool even a San Franciscan native into thinking they can leave their nighttime layers at home, I gather my friends and pile them in the car—along with a few cooking utensils and enough food to last an entire day—and drive to the beach. My rules: we leave before noon and go on a weekday, when the beach can seem as quiet as a church on Friday night.

One of my favorite things about dining outdoors in a warmer season is that it frees hands and bares skin. Winter's gloves and mittens have been packed into boxes and spring coats are traded for even lighters jackets, sweaters, or even better, nothing at all. This comes in handy for a beach picnic. When we don't need to wear or carry heavy clothing, our bodies feels lighter and our hands are freed for other things—better, important things. Like carrying bottles of rosé; bags of stone fruit, fish, and clams; and a simple kettle and tiny grill for a quiet, all-day beach excursion. Then we can eat well.

*There's no rush. When time is ample and the sky is clear, cooking can—
and should—take all day, with many requisite breaks.*

Some embrace summer for the very reason that it liberates them from cooking. Sometimes I do, too. At home, green beans only need a quick steam before getting tossed in vinaigrette and topped with walnuts and *queso blanco*. Heirloom tomatoes only need to be sliced and drizzled with olive oil before being wedged between crusty bread with a leftover grilled piece of flank steak from yesterday's dinner. But other times, like when I'm at the beach with loved ones, I embrace summer for the very cooking and eating style that it brings to food affairs. There's no rush. When time is ample and the sky is clear, cooking can—and should—take all day, with many requisite breaks.

It's during these snail-paced hours that I gain a greater understanding of the role of both cooking and food in our social life. Summer lets us reconsider our intentions for eating with others: to pass time and bond by sharing comfortable, nourishing space, food, and conversation.

When dusk seems to last for hours at the ocean, I'm never hurried to finish cooking. There's no sauce on the stove or dessert in the oven to mind. I never need to halt conversations with someone I care about to prepare another dish, for I can take my toes from the sand and walk over to the table to slice the next apricot course to share anytime I want. It can wait. Summer's catches, even fish, are happily eaten warm or cool when we're on the beach.

Although there's something blissful about walking along the beach in winter, bundled up, with a warm cup of coffee in your hand, the pace is always quicker. When it's warm, there's time for contemplation and slow walks. With its simple food, easy attire, and extended hours, summer allows us a different sort of peace and deliberation, one I want to last as long as possible. ○ ○ ○

# CHICKEN HARVEST

*In a world where my food is handled by hundreds of hands I have never shaken,
I find peace of mind in knowing that mine are the only to have touched
what I will soon savor.*

The sun rises on our rooster's early morning song. His cadence is rhythmic and full of promise for the day ahead; he is the voice for his flock of hens in the nesting boxes below. After climbing down from his high perch, he waits for me impatiently, pacing back and forth. He then peeks through the door and signals his ladies to follow. Merry hens greet me with warmth and vigor, and the feeling is mutual as I open each nesting box to find an egg in varied shades: soft turquoise, green, and blue. Just as I feel excitement when I receive the perfect Christmas gift, my heart still flutters at the sight of a new egg— every single time. To return the gift, I present an armload of fowl delicacies: chard, citrus, grains, and uprooted garden kale. My offerings are appreciated, but what grows beyond their nest is what truly satisfies my flock.

From the doors of the coop, the chickens explore the land, foraging the soil for sprightly bugs and rejoicing in the occasional kismet of a found caterpillar. It seems to me that chickens believe in the possibility of luck. There is no promise that a bug will be easily uncovered, yet I see in their approach that the chickens have total faith in the hunt. Enamored by their methods, I find myself wanting to be a part of the flock. A satiated hen makes her way over to me and, putting her instincts on pause, she nestles into the crook of my arm. Warmed by my body, she beats to the drum of my human hum. We find a comforting language, uncomplicated by words, in simply breathing together.

Truth be told, it was the thought of raising chickens that first sparked the dream of owning a farm. Before our house even had a working kitchen, we had thirty pullets in a brooder. I found dresses with extra-large pockets so a chick or two could be my companion on farm-chore walks. Occasionally, a few were even invited inside to witness the household happenings. From fluff to feathers, the flock has grown along with our farm, helping to shape us into the stewards we hoped to be.

While the chickens feed my soul with their abundance of life, they also provide nourishment for my family. In the act of harvesting our chickens I feel a connection with my ancestors who, not so long ago, practiced this skills as a means of survival. In a way, this is how I survive in a modern world—one ruled by the microwaves and takeout on speed dial. The task of plucking each and every feather is not a burden but a privilege. In a world where my food is handled by a hundred hands that I have never shaken, I find peace of mind in knowing that mine are the only to have touched what I will soon savor.

A bursting bouquet of rosemary, young spring onions, and thyme fills the inside of the bird, replenishing the life that once was. I slowly bake the chicken in a fragrant white wine base. As I set the table for our feast, my family is drawn in by the intoxicating scents—a loving tribute to the flora and fauna that surrounds us. The flavor of our bird challenges what I've always known as "poultry" with a cornucopia of tastes that unravel on our palates. I savor the culmination of my garden kale and orange rinds deep within the flavors of the meat. Then, resting my body after the meal, I listen for my rooster's song to awake me, yet again.

WORDS BY MEGAN MARTIN & PHOTOGRAPH BY ALPHA SMOOT

# PORTLAND, OR

### WORDS BY JULIE POINTER & PHOTOGRAPHS BY LAURA D'ART

Our first dinner was held in Portland, Oregon, where we gathered like family around hand-hewn tables. The evidence of makers was present, with wood, reupholstery, and leather-working studios surrounding us. The space itself was intimate, lived-in, and warm, with a generous skylight above, and we had a rare day of January sun that blessed the room. The meal felt like a homecoming; everyone hugged upon arrival, and pitched in to prepare the table before our meal. There was a palpable sense of joy as people began to greet each other and simultaneously share food—guests shook hands while passing plates to be served. We bestowed each other with shared gladness, which is a real and particular kind of gift, because it invites us to be present to the moment and to delight in what we have before us.

The most satisfying thing about the meal was seeing the work—and tangible generosity—of artists before us: winemakers, chefs, coffee-roasters, distillers, tea masters, music makers, floral arrangers, and photographers, among others. The abundance of gifts at our dinner was humbling, and prompted us to linger longer, listening to the stories of our tablemates. As the natural light diminished, the flickering votives stepped in as our hearth, encouraging soft conversation and the relishing of good company, just as it was meant to be: *con pane* (with bread). *Thank you to our Portland partners on page 138.*

# OUR INDIAN SUMMERS

WORDS BY AUSTIN SAILSBURY

PHOTOS COURTESY OF KANAKUK KAMP & WISCONSIN HISTORICAL SOCIETY

*At camp we didn't have to wear shoes much, but we wore bliss and we wore mischief.*

When our parents dropped us off at summer camp, they saw the rows of wooden cabins and the smiling staff; they saw the oak trees arching over the gravel road that led down to the lake and the beat-up camp trucks; they saw the piles of trunks packed with bug spray and swim goggles. They saw campers running every which way chasing footballs, Frisbees, and Gypsy, the faithful camp retriever. They saw the ever-present tribe of girl campers braiding each other's hair and whispering secrets and shooing away spies who tried to interfere. Then there was always the tinny sound of cheerful music playing over the PA, the brightly colored flags hanging overhead, and the general atmosphere of a backwoods carnival. To them this was, basically, camp.

When our parents dropped us off at camp they saw a well-oiled machine: people, property, and programs all working together in the spirit of clean-cut American optimism. What they didn't see, at least not directly, was the magic that came to life as soon as the last minivan or station wagon left the camp gates—the kind of magic that only comes to life in a place where there are cliffs to jump from, campfires to gather around, and tribal ceremonies to perform. The kind of magic that only happens when moms and dads are absent. They too might have experienced the camp magic when they were children—and maybe even longed to experience it once again—but they could not. They were adults now and had to buy insurance and pay for something called a mortgage. When our parents dropped

us off, they saw the face and shook the hand of camp, but only us kids felt its heartbeat and saw it come fully alive under long days of sunshine and the cloudless cerulean sky of our youth.

For those of us who went to camp year after year, summer was the nucleus around which the whole calendar circled. We believed camp was the best place on Earth (or anywhere else for that matter)—our own private Neverland. Except for video games, camp had everything we could ever want in life: tree houses and ball fields, a lake full of boats, bows and arrows and rifles, card tricks, and unlimited peanut butter sandwiches. At camp we didn't have to wear shoes much, but we wore bliss and we wore mischief.

There in the woods beside the lake, we found a place of profound simplicity, but also of expansive imagination. We were happy castaways who evolved into something perhaps less civilized but substantially more alive than what we were back in the suburbs. There, on a hill named for an Indian chief, we succeeded and failed in the arenas of competition. We bestowed nicknames upon one another. We broke things and built things. We idolized our counselors, those elder statesmen of outdoor do-goodery. We tried our hands at chivalry. We dressed as pirates and spoke in codes. We played the part of little brothers and big sisters and, if we could find the courage, the bravest of us even dared to dance with a member of the opposite sex.

But of all the memories from all my years at camp, there is one that stands alone in its clarity

*We were happy castaways who evolved into something perhaps less civilized but substantially more alive than what we were in the suburbs.*

and sacredness, one memory that lives with me as a moment of truest perfection. Because it is a ghost of happiness past, it can never be destroyed or undone—it stands like a lighthouse in my childhood, casting a searchlight over other foggy and darker memories. Even today if I close my eyes the scene materializes immediately and I can see it—I see us, sitting there near the cold lake, gathered around a roaring fire. I can see Rudy and B. Rob and Chris Minor and "Scharr Daddy" and all the boys sitting on railroad ties, weaving tall tales. I see their freckles and well-beaten tennis shoes, their sunburned skin, and the fire reflected in their eyes. I can hear us teasing Rudy. I can hear him tease us back. I can see the fiery dust flying upward each time we stir the coals and I can see kids drawing hieroglyphs in the sand at their feet. I can smell the smoke and seared sugar of lost marshmallows. I can smell that singular "lake smell" drifting over the camp road. How many hours did we sit there? How many times did we gather and spin the yarn of our own mythology, our own greatness? How much did we laugh at each other's clumsiness and our own lame jokes? I can see us then: both innocent and mean, fearless and terrified. We sat together around that campfire first as little boys and then as adolescents and then as

young men. Like a pilgrimage to the holy forest was summer camp; like a counsel of mighty chieftains were we around the campfire. There in the immortality of memory live the finest moments of my youth, spent with the greatest friends I've ever known.

The kids back at home, who never went to camp, never understood us—not the inside jokes or the camp legends or the songs. They didn't understand the value of the "Best All-Around Athlete" ribbons that hung on our walls or why we treasured the hand-written letters that came from old counselors and cabin-mates. Mostly, our friends back home were shocked that we would choose to live for a month without air-conditioning. Camp was an enigma to outsiders and we liked it that way. For kids from the suburbs, camp was our Narnia—once experienced it needed no explanation—but you had to step through the wardrobe to "get it." There we met fantastic characters, set out upon great adventures, and always came home a bit wiser and braver and taller than when we had left.

Whatever it cost our parents to send us to camp all those years, it was worth it. Their investments have paid us back with the immeasurable richness of a lifetime of golden summer memories that burn warmly through all seasons. ○ ○ ○

# BROOKLYN, NY

WORDS BY JULIE POINTER & PHOTOGRAPHS BY LEO PATRONE

**B**rooklyn emanates an energy that can be frenzied, frenetic, and crazy-making, but this same effervescence can be channeled into collaborative magic; then, a pocket of quiet calm descends on the city. We felt this sense of surprising tranquility at our meal in the open, lofty Green Building—though we were not subdued, but rather lulled into happy contentment by a perfectly satisfying feast, a sunlit table, and a room filled with warm, inspiring souls. The dinner and the social that followed were the whirlwind result of countless hands preparing, chopping, slicing, crafting, wrapping, arranging, and most of all, giving. The open-handedness of those involved in this gathering is what gave the evening a spirit of restful joy. It fed and nourished us, and encouraged us to give to one another, whether through the physicality of something we made, or by sharing ourselves across the table. Everyone came as a ready offering to their tablemates.

This attitude of gift-giving can alter a place, and it clearly poured over and out of every person present. We were graced with the generous provision of good things from around the city (primarily from neighborhoods within Brooklyn): chocolate, cheese, soap, sweet treats, greens, and timeless drinks, which we happily delighted in and gave thanks for. Even while the room filled with additional faces and the darkening day's shadows, the spirit of the space remained intact—a warm respite celebrating the work of many hands, inviting all to present themselves to the community surrounding them. *Thank you to our Brooklyn partners on page 138.*

# DINNER BOX

A PHOTO ESSAY BY JILL THOMAS

*While it can be hard to remember, my husband and I try to take a photo at dinners or meals that are special for us—a weekend getaway, our anniversary—then make an effort to actually print them to keep in a small box as a collection: our dinner box. We've done it for a couple years now, and it's fun for us to flip through and think of each specific meal with a short note on the back of them to help us remember.*

# TABLE TALK

*Table talk can be witty and stimulating, but more often than not, it is much more low-key; it is always, though, about sharing and shared experience.*

King Arthur famously gathered his knights around a table, and Thomas Jefferson hashed out some of his nascent country's most critical compromises not in a stateroom, but around his dining room table. Recent studies have shown that even the most humble of these fixtures—the household kitchen table—can make us happier, healthier, and even smarter, if we just gather there.

What is it about sitting down to a table? As we draw our chairs close, something happens: we talk. Maybe it's the leveling of gazes, or the unifying purpose of eating and drinking. Maybe it's the expanse of shared, common space. Maybe it's the mere fact that you can't escape: unlike cocktail party chit-chat, conversation can't end at a dinner table when you spot a friend across the room. Sitting down to a table is a commitment, whether for a ten-minute bowl of cereal or a long-lingering supper.

Discussion around the communal table takes many forms. Table talk can be witty and stimulating, but more often than not, it is much more low-key; it is always, though, about sharing and shared experience. For some, the dinner table might be the only place they can talk about their day, or hear about their partner's or kid's day.

For others, it's weekend brunch that allows time for the slow catching-up that weekdays may not allow. The recounting of daily life over the table allows us to focus our attention. I'll never forget entering the house of dear friends, bursting with news, and being urged to wait until dinner to tell the story—not because they were unexcited to hear the details, but because they wanted to be able to relish them, fully attentive to me.

The table can also become an intersection of two journeys. How many of us have sat down alone at a café, only to look up when we hear, "Is anyone sitting here?" Travelers enter the crossroads as strangers, then go their separate ways, having learned a little something about one another they can take with them.

Table talk can be internal, too. A solitary meal is an intimate act. Alone at the table—which means no phones computers, or even reading material—we allow ourselves to be nourished and attentive to our own thoughts.

In French, the call to eat the evening meal is not "Dinner!" but instead "*À table!*"—a distinction that should not be lost on us. When invited to eat or drink, we're not simply being summoned. The call to the table is so much more.

**WORDS BY SARAH SEARLE & PHOTOGRAPHS BY WILLIAM HEREFORD**

# HAVEN'S KITCHEN

WORDS BY KATIE SEARLE-WILLIAMS & PHOTOGRAPHS BY NICOLE FRANZEN

**B**ased in Manhattan, just two blocks from Union Square, Haven's Kitchen is everything its name suggests. Located in an idyllic carriage house adorned with white subway tiles, amidst rooms of iron- and white-colored accents paired with repurposed, centuries-old wood flooring, Haven's Kitchen functions as a multi-purpose operation: a cooking school, a specialty food shop, and an event space.

Founder Alison Schneider says that the aim of Haven's Kitchen is to educate community members about "delicious food that sustains people and our environment, while increasing the demand for locally and sustainably grown produce." Alison and her team, Lela Ilyinsky, Katie Fagan, and Julia Sullivan, bring together a solid variety of skills to create a haven of sustainable eating.

Aside from the myriad of hands-on classes, lectures, and demonstrations constantly available at Haven's Kitchen, you'll find monthly Supper Clubs where attendees experience communal-style dining, seasonal food, and great company.

The empowering philosophy of Haven's Kitchen's undeniably permeates throughout their work and space. They are true believers that personal wellness and the well-being of our planet are intricately and permanently connected. To find out more and become involved with Haven's Kitchen, visit their website www.havenskitchen.com.

# DINNER DISCUSSION 33

*Some people collect items; Leif collects dinner companions.*

The tide is high when we reach Julie Kahn's compact, two-story houseboat in Sausalito. It's a treat to be invited onto one of these floating homes and we're all a little giddy just taking in the surroundings. So it's not until the first subtle lull in conversation—after a round of introductions have been made, drinks have been offered and accepted, and a few nuggets of cheese and some citrus-scented olives have been eaten—that someone points out the motion of the floor swaying beneath us. Before long we all feel it. And the incessant rocking, combined with the pomegranate Bellinis we've been handed—with the fruit's deep red seeds floating in the glass—makes for a light-headed first hour.

We graze as our chef and convener, Leif Hedendal, prepares a delicate, three-course lunch. He is quiet and focused when he's cooking, a kind of anti-host who artfully sets up a vacuum and let's the group fill the space, all the while listening from the sidelines.

Some people collect items; Leif collects dinner companions. Every month for the last three years he has made his dream dinner party list. He thinks big, including a range of activists, artists, writers, filmmakers, farmers, and musicians he's met, read about, or encountered in some way. Then—and here's what sets him apart from the rest of us—Leif simply invites them to join him for what he calls a Dinner Discussion. Contrary to how it sounds, though, there is never an assigned topic, nor are there any rules about how the discussion should unravel. The meal is always local, seasonal, eclectic, and intuitive (Leif's menus are lyrical lists of ingredients, and he often decides how to prepare the meal as he's going along). He keeps a very simple blog documenting the meals; he lists the date, the guests' names, and the menu, and he shares only a handful of photos (often just one) of the night. To see the lists alone you might think this is some kind of networking event, but the meals couldn't feel further from that. Guests simply eat, chat (or observe), and go home feeling a little more connected and a little more cared for.

For this thirty-third Dinner Discussion (which is actually a lunch), we are lucky to have the kind of rare, sunny day in late November that will allow us to eat lunch on Julie's second-floor deck, where the bay is visible on one side and the hills of the Marin Headlands on the other. The artists—Amy Franceschini, Stijn Schiffeleers, Susanne Cockrell, and *Ted Purves*—outnumber the rest of us. Filmmaker Les Blank, in his 80s, is the oldest among us and serves as a kind of guest of honor. He tells us about the film for which he's been collecting footage for the last fourteen years, and he shares his favorite recipe (sardines wrapped in grape leaves foraged from a neighbor's vine).

There's an arc to the meal that I recognize from the last time I attended a Dinner Discussion: first we are all a little awkward and expectant, then we all allow ourselves to get fully absorbed in the meal together (the highlight of this one was a nettle puree served with roasted onions, sunchokes, and chanterelle mushrooms), until finally we are so relaxed that we start talking and joking together like a group of old friends. We stay until the sun has dropped behind the hills and the tide has begun to recede again, to make its way home like the rest of us.

WORDS BY TWILIGHT GREENAWAY & PHOTOGRAPH BY MATTHEW REAMER
FOOD AND STYLING BY LEIF HEDENDAL

# FROM THE GARDEN

WORDS AND PHOTOGRAPHS BY ALICE GAO

*As my dad hoses down the bunches in the sink, soil gives way to reveal*
*a freshness you only get from growing your own.*

---

In the summer, my favorite meals are the ones completely grown, harvested, and cooked by my parents. I often boast to my fellow city dweller friends that in the summer, my parents never have to go grocery shopping. In their modest backyard, where there used to be a swimming pool, they have transformed a plot of land into a thriving patch of good eating.

My mom is usually in the garden when I arrive. Her straw hat is the only visible part of her among the tomato cages, thick vines, and corn stalks (yes, corn—you read that right). Eventually, she emerges triumphantly, carrying a basket overflowing with greens and reds. She spreads them out for me to admire, and I notice the striking veins of the leaves. I nibble on some edible flowers, introducing my palate to a surprisingly peppery flavor. As my dad hoses down the bunches in the sink, soil gives way to reveal a freshness you only get from growing your own.

Their routine is enviable. Within an hour of picking through the garden, cooked dishes arrive on the table. Simple dishes highlighting each vegetable are all we need and crave during these hot months. There is little greater satisfaction than knowing the source of your meal is a stone's throw out the window—and of course, they send me back to the city with more bags than I can manage of all their summer bounty. ○ ○ ○

**SPECIAL THANKS**
*Paintings* Katie Stratton
*Art Director at Weldon Owen* Ali Zeigler
*Production Director at Weldon Owen*
Chris Hemesath

**COVER PHOTO**
*Photographer* Young & Hungry

**RENAISSANCE JUICING**
*Photo Assistant* James Fitzgerald

**DINING FOR ONE**
*Location* communalrestaurant.com
*Pictured* thinkinginshapes.com

**SUMMER LIST PHOTOGRAPH**
*Photographer* Young & Hungry

**INN BY THE SEA**
marstonhouse.com

**BELLOCQ TEA ATELIER**
*Prop stylist* Shane Powers

**INTO BEGUILING WILD**
*Location* Vancouver Island, Canada
*Props* Herriott Grace & Lark
*Production* Nikole Herriott
*Michael Graydon* is a photographer who loves camping and baseball and believes that life is best done in collaboration.

*Nikole Herriott* is half the partnership behind the popular housewares brand Herriott Grace and is the words behind the well-known blog Forty-sixth at Grace.

*Tara O'Brady* is a freelance food writer and the creator of the acclaimed food blog seven spoons.

They all live in, or near, Toronto, Ontario.

**MOUNTAIN RESPITE**
*Food Stylist* Maria del Mar Sacasa
*Props & Wardrobe* Emma Robertson &
Jessica Comingore
*Video* Steve Pappin
*Producer* Christin Rose
*Prop Loans* Yeah Rentals

**OUR INDIAN SUMMERS**
*First Two Photos Courtesy of* Kanakuk Kamp
*The following photos courtesy of* Wisconsin Historical Society: WHI-80890, WHI-61121, WHI-43120, WHI-81198.

**TABLE TALK**
*Equipment Rental* FotoCare
*Prop Loans* Canvas
*Photo Assistant* Peter Duong
*Food Stylist* Rebekah Peppler
*Prop Stylist* Alyssa Pagano
*Talent* Alex Strada, Rose Gold,
Andrew Karp, Tucker Pawlick

**ENDNOTES**

1 Annie Dillard, *Pilgrim at Tinker Creek* (New York: Harper Perennial Modern Classics, 1974), 33.

2 From TRAVELS WITH CHARLEY by John Steinbeck, copyright (c) 1961, 1962 by The Curtis Publishing Co., (c) 1962 by John Steinbeck, renewed (c) 1990 by Elaine Steinbeck, Thom Steinbeck, and John Steinbeck IV. Used by permission of Viking Penguin, a division of Penguin Group (USA) Inc.

**BACK COVER QUOTE CREDIT**
Mitch Albom, *Tuesdays With Morrie* (New York, New York: Doubleday, 1997), 157.

WWW.KINFOLKMAG.COM

# KEEP IN TOUCH

**THANKS TO OUR DINNER SERIES PARTNERS:**

**PORTLAND**
*Antica Terra Winery*
*Beam & Anchor*
*Chasity Glass*
*Emerald Petals*
*Foxfire Teas*
*Greylag*
*Heart Roasters*
*House Spirits Distillery*
*Laura D'Art*
*Oncology Youth Connection*
*Paul Searle*
*Skin & Bones Bistro*
*Spartan*
*Type A Press*
*West Elm*

**BROOKLYN**
*Amy's Bread*
*Amy Merrick*
*Ariel Dearie*
*Art in the Age Craft Spirits*
*The Big Cheese*
*Blue Moon Acres*
*Brooklyn Brewery*
*Brooklyn Oenology*
*Brooklyn Slate*
*Crumpler*
*Frances Palmer Pottery*
*The Green Building*
*Honey of a Thousand Flowers*
*Honey Ridge Farms*
*Jarlsberg*
*Jewels of New York*
*Karlsson's*
*Leo Patrone*
*Mast Brothers Chocolate*
*Palomino*
*Pushcart Coffee*
*Saipua*
*Smoked Meat NY*
*The Stand*
*Type A Press*
*Vs the Brain*
*West Elm*
*Woolwich Dairy*